RABINDRANATH
TAGORE

LEGENDS AND LEGACIES

THE BIOGRAPHY OF
RABINDRANATH
TAGORE

Published by
Rupa Publications India Pvt. Ltd 2024
7/16, Ansari Road, Daryaganj
New Delhi 110002

Sales centres:
Bengaluru Chennai
Hyderabad Jaipur Kathmandu
Kolkata Mumbai Prayagraj

Copyright © Rupa Publications India Pvt. Ltd 2024

The views and opinions expressed in this book are the author's own and the facts are as reported by him which have been verified to the extent possible, and the publishers are not in any way liable for the same.

All rights reserved.
No part of this publication may be reproduced, transmitted, or stored in a retrieval system, in any form or by any means, electronic, mechanical, photocopying, recording or otherwise, without the prior permission of the publisher.

P-ISBN: 978-93-6156-417-8
E-ISBN: 978-93-6156-038-5

First impression 2024

10 9 8 7 6 5 4 3 2 1

Printed in India

This book is sold subject to the condition that it shall not, by way of trade or otherwise, be lent, resold, hired out, or otherwise circulated, without the publisher's prior consent, in any form of binding or cover other than that in which it is published.

Contents

Introduction	7
Rabindranath Tagore	9
Tagore's upbringing and early influences	11
Works of Tagore	22
Tagore's political views, educational philosophy, and legacy	33
Selected Quotes of Rabindranath Tagore	37
Interview of Tagore with Einstein: Meeting of two great minds	51
Tagore and Cinema	57
Foundations of Tagore's Philosophy	63
Excerpts from Tagore's most famous creation, Gitanjali	66
List of works	78

Introduction

Hey there, curious minds!

Have you ever heard of a magical poet who could weave words into enchanting songs and stories? Let me introduce you to Rabindranath Tagore, a true literary superhero! He didn't have a cape or superpowers, but his pen was mightier than any sword, and his words inspired millions across the globe.

Imagine growing up in a bustling mansion filled with music, art, and literature. That's where young Rabindranath spent his childhood in Jorasanko, Kolkata. Born into a family of intellectuals and artists, he was surrounded by creativity and brilliance from the start. His father was a philosopher, and his mother nurtured his love for poetry. Even though he didn't attend school in the traditional sense, Tagore was a curious and avid learner, exploring the vast world of knowledge through books and life experiences.

Here's a charming thought from Tagore that captures his poetic spirit: "Let your life lightly dance on the edges of Time like dew on the tip of a leaf." Beautiful, isn't it? He believed in the beauty of simplicity and the profound wisdom hidden in nature.

Tagore's journey wasn't just about writing poems; he was also a philosopher, artist, playwright, and a tireless advocate for education and social reform. He founded Visva-Bharati University, a place where learning went beyond textbooks, blending the best of Eastern and Western philosophies. Imagine a school where you could learn under the shade of trees, surrounded by nature's splendour—that was Tagore's vision for education.

One of his most significant achievements was winning the Nobel Prize for Literature in 1913 for his collection of poems, "Gitanjali." Picture this: a poet from India captivating the world with his soulful verses, bringing together hearts and minds across continents. That's the kind of magic Tagore created with his words.

Here's another gem from Tagore that might make you smile: "You can't cross the sea merely by standing and staring at the water." It's a gentle nudge to dive into life, embrace challenges, and follow your dreams with courage and determination.

Rabindranath Tagore wasn't just a poet; he was a beacon of light in a world often clouded by darkness. His songs, stories, and ideas continue to inspire generations, reminding us of the timeless beauty of dreams and the power of creativity. Do you know - India's National Gallery of Modern Art lists 102 works by Tagore in its collections.

So, dear young explorers, let's take a leaf out of Tagore's book—dream big, stay curious, and let your life be a melody that resonates with joy and wisdom. Just like Tagore, you, too, can weave your own stories and leave a lasting impact on the world!

1

Rabindranath Tagore

Rabindranath Tagore 7 May 1861 – 7 August 1941, sobriquet Gurudev, was a Bengali polymath who reshaped Bengali literature and music, as well as Indian art with Contextual Modernism in the late 19th and early 20th centuries. Author of Gitanjali and its 'profoundly sensitive, fresh and beautiful verse', he became in 1913 the first non-European to win the Nobel Prize in Literature. Tagore's poetic songs were viewed as spiritual and mercurial; however, his 'elegant prose and magical poetry' remain largely unknown outside Bengal. He is sometimes referred to as 'the Bard of Bengal'.

A Pirali Brahmin from Calcutta with ancestral gentry roots in Jessore, Tagore wrote poetry as an eight-year-old. At the age of sixteen, he released his first substantial poems under the pseudonym Bhanusiṃha ('Sun Lion'), which were seized upon by literary authorities as long-lost classics. By 1877 he graduated to his first short stories and dramas, published under his real name. As a humanist, universalist internationalist,

Head Painting by Rabindranath Tagore
Credits: Post of India, GODL-India <https://data.gov.in/sites/default/files/Gazette_Notification_OGDL.pdf>, via Wikimedia Commons

and ardent anti-nationalist, he denounced the British Raj and advocated independence from Britain. As an exponent of the Bengal Renaissance, he advanced a vast canon that comprised paintings, sketches and doodles, hundreds of texts, and some two thousand songs; his legacy also endures in the institution he founded, Visva-Bharati University.

Tagore modernized Bengali art by spurning rigid classical forms and resisting linguistic strictures. His novels, stories, songs, dance-dramas, and essays spoke to topics political and personal. Gitanjali (Song Offerings), Gora (Fair-Faced) and Ghare-Baire (The Home and the World) are his best-known works, and his verse, short stories, and novels were acclaimed—or panned—for their lyricism, colloquialism, naturalism, and unnatural contemplation. His compositions were chosen by two nations as national anthems: India's Jana Gana Mana and Bangladesh's Amar Shonar Bangla. The Sri Lankan national anthem was inspired by his work.

> **Fun Fact:**
> **Visiting Insomniac:**
> Tagore often suffered from insomnia, leading him to write some of his most profound works during sleepless nights.

2

Tagore's upbringing and early influences

Early life: 1861–1878

The youngest of thirteen surviving children, Tagore (nicknamed 'Rabi') was born on 7 May 1861 in the Jorasanko mansion in Calcutta to Debendranath Tagore (1817–1905) and Sarada Devi (1830–1875).

Tagore was raised mostly by servants; his mother had died in his early childhood and his father travelled widely. The Tagore family was at the forefront of the Bengal renaissance. They hosted the publication of literary magazines; theatre and recitals of Bengali and Western classical music featured there regularly. Tagore's father invited several professional Dhrupad musicians to stay in the house and teach Indian classical music to the children. Tagore's oldest brother Dwijendranath was a philosopher and poet. Another brother, Satyendranath, was the first Indian appointed to the elite and formerly all-European Indian Civil Service. Yet another brother, Jyotirindranath, was a musician, composer, and playwright. His sister Swarnakumari became a novelist. Jyotirindranath's wife Kadambari Devi, slightly older than Tagore, was a dear

> **Fun Fact:**
> **Boat School:** Tagore conceptualised a floating school on a boat to reach children in remote areas along the Ganges River.

> **Fun Fact:**
> Santiniketan's curriculum was holistic, integrating physical, intellectual, and spiritual growth through nature walks, open-air classes, and creative arts, fostering a deep connection with the environment and encouraging lifelong learning.

friend and powerful influence. Her abrupt suicide in 1884, soon after he married, left him profoundly distraught for years.

Tagore largely avoided classroom schooling and preferred to roam the manor or nearby Bolpur and Panihati, which the family visited. His brother Hemendranath tutored and physically conditioned him—by having him swim the Ganges or trek through hills, by gymnastics, and by practicing judo and wrestling. He learned drawing, anatomy, geography and history, literature, mathematics, Sanskrit, and English—his least favourite subject. Tagore loathed formal education—his scholarly travails at the local Presidency College spanned a single day. Years later he held that proper teaching does not explain things; proper teaching stokes curiosity:

After his upanayan (coming-of-age) rite at age eleven, Tagore and his father left Calcutta in February 1873 to tour India for several months, visiting his father's Shantiniketan estate and Amritsar before reaching the Himalayan hill station of Dalhousie. There Tagore read biographies, studied history, astronomy, modern science, and Sanskrit, and examined the classical poetry of Kalidasa. During his 1-month stay at Amritsar in 1873 he was greatly influenced by melodious gurbani and nanak bani being sung at Golden Temple for which both father and son were regular visitors. He mentions about this in his *'MY REMINISCENCES (1912)*

> **Fun Fact:**
> Festivals like Basant Utsav are integral to Santiniketan's educational philosophy, fostering community and cultural heritage. These events unify students, teachers, and locals, emphasizing shared cultural values and artistic expression.

The golden temple of Amritsar comes back to me like a dream. Many a morning have I accompanied my father to this Gurudarbar of the Sikhs in the middle of the lake. There the sacred chanting resounds continually. My father, seated amidst the throng of worshippers, would sometimes add his voice to the hymn of praise, and finding a stranger joining in their devotions they would wax enthusiastically cordial, and we would return loaded with the sanctified offerings of sugar crystals and other sweets.

He wrote 6 poems relating to Sikhism and a number of articles in Bengali child magazine about Sikhism.

Tagore returned to Jorosanko and completed a set of major works by 1877, one of them a long poem in the Maithili style of Vidyapati. As a joke, he claimed that these were the lost works of (what he claimed was) a newly discovered 17th-century Vaiṣṇava poet Bhānusiṃha. Regional experts accepted them as the lost works of Bhānusiṃha. He debuted in the short-story genre in Bengali with 'Bhikharini' ('The Beggar Woman'). Published in the same year, Sandhya Sangit (1882) includes the poem 'Nirjharer Swapnabhanga' ('The Rousing of the Waterfall').

Fun Fact:
Tagore's model blended Eastern and Western educational philosophies, promoting exploration and interaction with the world. This approach included flexible schedules adapting to natural changes, integrating nature walks, and excursions.

Shelaidaha: 1878–1901

Because Debendranath wanted his son to become a barrister, Tagore enrolled at a public school in Brighton, East Sussex, England in 1878. He stayed for several months at a house that the Tagore family owned near Brighton and Hove, in Medina Villas; in 1877 his nephew and niece—Suren and Indira Devi, the children of Tagore's brother Satyendranath—were sent together with

Rabindranath Tagore and Mrinalini Devi, 1883

their mother, Tagore's sister-in-law, to live with him. He briefly read law at University College London, but again left school, opting instead for independent study of Shakespeare's plays Coriolanus, and Antony and Cleopatra and the Religio Medici of Thomas Browne. Lively English, Irish, and Scottish folk tunes impressed Tagore, whose own tradition of Nidhubabu-authored kirtans and tappas and Brahmo hymnody was subdued. In 1880 he returned to Bengal degree-less, resolving to reconcile European novelty with Brahmo traditions, taking the best from each. After returning to Bengal, Tagore regularly published poems, stories, and novels. These had a profound impact within Bengal itself but received little national attention. In 1883 he married 10-year-old Mrinalini Devi, born Bhabatarini, 1873–1902 (this was a common practice at the time). They had five children, two of whom died in childhood.

In 1890 Tagore began managing his vast ancestral estates in Shelaidaha (today a region of Bangladesh); he was joined there by his wife and children in 1898. Tagore released his Manasi poems (1890), among his best-known work. As Zamindar Babu, Tagore criss-crossed the Padma River in command of the Padma, the luxurious family barge (also known as 'budgerow'). He collected mostly token rents and blessed villagers who in turn honoured him with banquets—occasionally of dried rice and sour milk. He met Gagan Harkara, through whom he became familiar with Baul Lalon Shah, whose folk songs greatly influenced Tagore. Tagore worked to popularise Lalon's songs. The period 1891–1895, Tagore's Sadhana period, named after one of his magazines, was his most productive; in these years he wrote more than half the stories of the three-volume, 84-story *Galpaguchchha*. Its ironic and grave tales examined the voluptuous poverty of an idealised rural Bengal.

Shantiniketan: 1901–1932
Middle years of Rabindranath Tagore

In 1901, Rabindranath Tagore moved to Shantiniketan to establish an ashram with a prayer hall, school, gardens, and a library. During this period, he faced personal losses and sustained himself financially through inheritance and modest book sales. He published Naivedya (1901) and Kheya (1906). In 1921, Tagore and Leonard Elmhirst founded the Institute for Rural Reconstruction, later known as Shriniketan, to revitalise rural communities, counter colonial impact, and support Dalits through education and self-help initiatives.

Tsinghua University, 1924

In 1901 Tagore moved to Shantiniketan to found an ashram with a marble-floored prayer hall—The Mandir—an experimental school, groves of trees, gardens, a library. There his wife and two of his children died. His father died in 1905. He received monthly payments as part of his inheritance and income from the Maharaja of Tripura, sales of his family's jewellery, his seaside bungalow in Puri, and a derisory 2,000 rupees in book royalties. He gained Bengali and foreign readers alike; he published *Naivedya* (1901) and *Kheya* (1906) and translated poems into free verse.

Rabindranath Tagore with His Granddaughter and Grandnephew in Shantiniketan on 10 April 1934

In November 1913, Tagore learned he had won that year's Nobel Prize in Literature: the Swedish Academy appreciated the idealistic—and for Westerners—accessible nature of a small body of his translated material focused on the 1912 *Gitanjali: Song Offerings*. He was awarded a knighthood by King George V in the 1915 Birthday Honours, but renounced it after the 1919 Jallianwala Bagh massacre.

In 1921, Tagore and agricultural economist Leonard Elmhirst set up the 'Institute for Rural Reconstruction', later renamed Shriniketan or 'Abode of Welfare', in Surul, a village near the ashram. With it, Tagore sought to moderate Gandhi's Swaraj protests, which he occasionally blamed for British India's perceived mental — and thus ultimately colonial — decline. He sought aid from donors, officials, and scholars worldwide to 'free villages from the shackles of helplessness and ignorance' by 'vitalizing knowledge'. In the early 1930s he targeted ambient 'abnormal caste consciousness' and untouchability. He lectured against these, he penned Dalit heroes for his poems and his dramas, and he campaigned—successfully— to open Guruvayoor Temple to Dalits.

Twilight years: 1932–1941
Germany, 1931

Tagore and Gandhi

Dutta and Robinson describe this phase of Tagore's life as being one of a 'peripatetic litterateur'. It affirmed his opinion that human divisions were shallow. During a May 1932 visit to a Bedouin encampment in the Iraqi desert, the tribal chief told him that *'Our prophet has said that a true Muslim is he by whose words and deeds not the least of his brother-men may ever come to any harm ...'* Tagore confided in his diary: *'I was startled into recognizing in his words the voice of essential humanity.'* To the end Tagore scrutinized orthodoxy—and in 1934, he struck. That year, an earthquake hit Bihar and killed thousands. Gandhi hailed it as seismic karma, as divine retribution avenging the oppression of Dalits. Tagore rebuked him for his seemingly ignominious implications. He mourned the perennial poverty of Calcutta and the socio-economic decline of Bengal, and detailed these newly plebeian aesthetics in an unrhymed hundred-line poem whose technique of searing double-vision foreshadowed Satyajit Ray's film *Apur Sansar*. Fifteen new volumes appeared, among them prose-poem works *Punashcha* (1932), *Shes Saptak* (1935), and *Patraput* (1936). Experimentation continued in his prose-songs and dance-dramas— *Chitra* (1914), *Shyama* (1939), and *Chandalika* (1938)— and in his novels— *Dui Bon* (1933), *Malancha* (1934), and *Char Adhyay* (1934).

> **Fun Fact:**
> Musical Explorer: Tagore composed over 2,000 songs (Rabindra Sangeet) in various styles, including traditional Bengali, Western classical, and even Middle Eastern influences.

Tagore's remit expanded to science in his last years, as hinted in Visva-Parichay, a 1937 collection of essays. His respect for scientific laws and his exploration of biology, physics, and astronomy informed his poetry, which exhibited extensive naturalism and verisimilitude. He wove the process of science, the narratives of scientists, into stories in Se (1937), Tin Sangi (1940), and Galpasalpa (1941). His last five years were marked by chronic pain and two long periods of illness. These began when Tagore lost consciousness in late 1937; he remained comatose and near death for a time. This was followed in late 1940 by a similar spell, from which he never recovered. Poetry from these valetudinary years is among his finest. A period of prolonged agony ended with Tagore's death on 7 August 1941, aged eighty; he was in an upstairs room of the Jorasanko mansion he was raised in. The date is still mourned. A. K. Sen, brother of the first chief election commissioner, received dictation from Tagore on 30 July 1941, a day prior to a scheduled operation.

Tagore and Mussolini
Credits: State Archive, Public domain, via Wikimedia Commons

His last poem.

I'm lost in the middle of my birthday. I want my friends, their touch, with the earth's last love. I will take life's final offering, I will take the human's last blessing. Today my sack is empty. I have given completely whatever I had to give. In return if I receive anything—some love, some forgiveness—then I will take it with me when I step on the boat that crosses to the festival of the wordless end.

Travels

Between 1878 and 1932, Tagore set foot in more than thirty countries on five continents. In 1912, he took a sheaf of his translated works to England, where they gained attention from missionary and Gandhi protégé Charles F. Andrews, Irish poet William Butler Yeats, Ezra Pound, Robert Bridges, Ernest Rhys, Thomas Sturge Moore, and others. Yeats wrote the preface to the English translation of *Gitanjali*; Andrews joined Tagore at Shantiniketan. In November 1912 Tagore began touring the United States and the United Kingdom, staying in Butterton, Staffordshire with Andrews's clergymen friends. From May 1916 until April 1917, he lectured in Japan and the United States. He denounced nationalism. His essay *'Nationalism in India'* was scorned and praised; it was admired by Romain Rolland and other pacifists.

Shortly after returning home, the 63-year-old Tagore accepted an invitation from the Peruvian government. He travelled to Mexico. Each government pledged US$100,000 to his school to commemorate the visits. A week after his 6 November 1924 arrival in Buenos Aires, an ill Tagore shifted to the Villa Miralrío at the behest of Victoria Ocampo. He left for home in January 1925. In May 1926 Tagore reached Naples; the next day he met Mussolini in Rome. Their warm rapport ended when Tagore pronounced upon Il Duce's fascist finesse. He had earlier enthused: *'without any doubt he is a great personality. There is such a massive vigour in that head that it reminds one of Michael Angelo's chisel.'* A *'fire-bath'* of fascism was to have educed *'the immortal soul of Italy ... clothed in quenchless light'*.

Rabindranath Tagore during his time in England
Credits: Visva-Bharati Granthana Vibhaga

On 14 July 1927 Tagore and two companions began a four-month tour of Southeast Asia. They visited Bali, Java, Kuala Lumpur, Malacca, Penang, Siam, and Singapore. The resultant travelogues compose *Jatri* (1929). In early 1930 he left Bengal for a nearly year-long tour of Europe and the United States. Upon returning to Britain—and as his paintings were exhibited in Paris and London—he lodged at a Birmingham Quaker settlement. He wrote his Oxford Hibbert Lectures and spoke at the annual London Quaker meet. There, addressing relations between the British and the Indians—a topic he would tackle repeatedly over the next two years—Tagore spoke of a *'dark chasm of aloofness'*. He visited Aga Khan III, stayed at Dartington Hall, toured Denmark, Switzerland, and Germany from June to mid-September 1930, then went on into the Soviet Union. In April 1932 Tagore, intrigued by the Persian mystic Hafez, was hosted by Reza Shah Pahlavi. In his other travels, Tagore interacted with Henri Bergson, Albert Einstein, Robert Frost, Thomas Mann, George Bernard Shaw, H.G. Wells, and Romain Rolland. Visits to Persia and Iraq (in 1932) and Sri Lanka (in 1933) composed Tagore's final foreign tour, and his dislike of communalism and nationalism only deepened. Vice-President of India M. Hamid Ansari has said that Rabindranath Tagore heralded the cultural rapprochement between communities, societies, and nations much before it became the liberal norm of conduct. Tagore was a man ahead of his time. He wrote in 1932, while on a visit to Iran, that *'each country of Asia will solve its own historical problems according to its strength, nature and needs, but the lamp they will each carry on their path to progress will converge to illuminate the common ray of knowledge.'*

Rabindranath Tagore Plaque - Gouripur House - Kalimpong
Credits: Sumit Surai, CC BY-SA 4.0 <https://creativecommons.org/licenses/by-sa/4.0>, via Wikimedia Commons

Kalimpong, a beautiful hill station in West Bengal, held great significance for Rabindranath Tagore. It served as both a refuge and a source of inspiration for him, leading to multiple visits to the area. Drawn by its peace and tranquility, Tagore composed numerous poems and essays while staying there. Gauripur House, where he resided during his visits, has since become a revered site for literary enthusiasts. The serene Himalayan setting of Kalimpong, coupled with Tagore's love of nature, profoundly influenced his pursuit of serenity and inspiration, as reflected in his literary works.

3

Works of Tagore

Known mostly for his poetry, Tagore wrote novels, essays, short stories, travelogues, dramas, and thousands of songs. Of Tagore's prose, his short stories are perhaps most highly regarded; he is indeed credited with originating the Bengali-language version of the genre. His works are frequently noted for their rhythmic, optimistic, and lyrical nature. Such stories mostly borrow from

Stamp of India (2011) - 150th Birth Anniversary of Rabindranath Tagore
Credits: Post of India

deceptively simple subject matter: commoners. Tagore's non-fiction grappled with history, linguistics, and spirituality. He wrote autobiographies. His travelogues, essays, and lectures were compiled into several volumes, including Europe *Jatrir Patro* (Letters from Europe) and *Manusher Dhormo* (The Religion of Man). His brief chat with gandhi, 'Note on the Nature of Reality', is included as an appendix to the latter. On the occasion of Tagore's 150th birthday an anthology (titled *Kalanukromik Rabindra Rachanabali*) of the total body of his works is currently being published in Bengali in chronological order. This includes all versions of each work and fills about eighty volumes. In 2011, Harvard University Press collaborated with Visva-Bharati University to publish The Essential Tagore, the largest anthology of Tagore's works available in English; it was edited by Fakrul Alam and Radha Chakravarthy and marks the 150th anniversary of Tagore's birth.

Drama

Tagore's experiences with drama began when he was sixteen, with his brother Jyotirindranath. He wrote his first original dramatic piece when he was twenty — Valmiki Pratibha which was shown at the Tagore's mansion. Tagore stated that his works sought to articulate 'the play of feeling and not of action'. In 1890 he wrote Visarjan (an adaptation of his novella Rajarshi), which has been regarded as his finest drama. In the original Bengali language, such works included intricate subplots and extended monologues. Later, Tagore's dramas used more philosophical and allegorical themes. The play *Dak Ghar* ('The Post Office'; 1912), describes the child Amal defying his stuffy and puerile confines by ultimately 'falling asleep', hinting his physical death. A story with borderless appeal—gleaning rave reviews in Europe—*Dak Ghar* dealt with death as, in Tagore's words, 'spiritual freedom' from 'the world of hoarded wealth and certified creeds'. Another is Tagore's *Chandalika* (Untouchable Girl), which was modelled on an ancient Buddhist legend describing how Ananda, the Gautama Buddha's disciple, asks a tribal girl for water. In Raktakarabi ('Red' or 'Blood Oleanders') is an allegorical struggle against a kleptocrat king who rules over the residents of Yaksha puri.

Valmiki Pratibha: Indira Devi, and Rabindranath Tagore

Chitrangada, Chandalika, and Shyama are other key plays that have dance-drama adaptations, which together are known as Rabindra Nritya Natya.

Short stories

Tagore began his career in short stories in 1877—when he was only sixteen—with '*Bhikharini*' ('The Beggar Woman'). With this, Tagore effectively invented the Bengali-language short story genre. The four years from 1891 to 1895 are known as Tagore's 'Sadhana' period (named for one of Tagore's magazines). This period was among Tagore's most fecund, yielding more than half the stories contained in the three-volume Galpaguchchha, which itself is a collection of eighty-four stories. Such stories usually showcase

Tagore's reflections upon his surroundings, on modern and fashionable ideas, and on interesting mind puzzles (which Tagore was fond of testing his intellect with). Tagore typically associated his earliest stories (such as those of the 'Sadhana' period) with an exuberance of vitality and spontaneity; these characteristics were intimately connected with Tagore's life in the common villages of, among others, Patisar, Shajadpur, and Shilaida while managing the Tagore family's vast landholdings. There, he beheld the lives of India's poor and common people; Tagore thereby took to examining their lives with a penetrative depth and feeling that was singular in Indian literature up to that point. In particular, such stories as '*Kabuliwala*' ('The Fruitseller from Kabul', published in 1892), '*Kshudita Pashan*' ('The Hungry Stones') (August 1895), and 'Atithi' ('The Runaway', 1895) typified this analytic focus on the downtrodden. Many of the other Galpaguchchha stories were written in Tagore's Sabuj Patra period from 1914 to 1917, also named after one of the magazines that Tagore edited and heavily contributed to.

> **Fun Fact:**
> Santiniketan's holistic curriculum integrates physical, intellectual, and spiritual growth, with students engaging in environmental activities and artistic pursuits. This blend of Eastern and Western philosophies fosters exploration and global cultural interaction.

Novels

Tagore wrote eight novels and four novellas, among them Chaturanga, Shesher Kobita, Char Odhay, and Noukadubi. Ghare Baire (The Home and the World)—through the lens of the idealistic zamindar protagonist Nikhil—excoriates rising Indian nationalism, terrorism, and religious zeal in the Swadeshi movement; a frank expression of Tagore's conflicted sentiments, it emerged from a 1914 bout of depression. The novel ends in Hindu-Muslim violence and Nikhil's—likely mortal—wounding.

Gora raises controversial questions regarding the Indian identity. As with Ghare Baire, matters of self-identity (jati), personal freedom, and religion are developed in the context of a family story and love triangle. In it an Irish boy orphaned in the Sepoy Mutiny is raised by Hindus as the titular gora—'whitey'. Ignorant of his foreign origins, he chastises Hindu religious backsliders out of love for the indigenous Indians and solidarity with them against his hegemon-compatriots. He falls for a Brahmo girl, compelling his worried foster father to reveal his lost past and cease his nativist zeal. As a 'true dialectic' advancing 'arguments for and against strict traditionalism', it tackles the colonial conundrum by 'portraying the value of all positions within a particular frame…not only syncretism, not only liberal orthodoxy, but the extremest reactionary traditionalism he defends by an appeal to what humans share.' Among these Tagore highlights 'identity… conceived of as dharma.'

> **Fun Fact:**
> Astrology Skeptic: Despite his spiritual leanings, Tagore was highly skeptical of astrology and often mocked it in his writings.

In Jogajog (Relationships), the heroine Kumudini—bound by the ideals of Siva-Sati, exemplified by Dakshayani—is torn between her pity for the sinking fortunes of her progressive and compassionate elder brother and his foil: her ruse of a husband. Tagore flaunts his feminist leanings; pathos depicts the plight and ultimate demise of women trapped by pregnancy, duty, and family honour; he simultaneously trucks with Bengal's putrescent landed gentry. The story revolves around the underlying rivalry between

> **Fun Fact:**
> Santiniketan's rural development focus uplifted local communities, integrating vocational training and promoting cottage industries. Sriniketan extends this mission, teaching sustainable agricultural practices and empowering local populations through education.

two families—the Chatterjee's, aristocrats now on the decline (Biprodas) and the Ghosals (Madhusudan), representing new money and new arrogance. Kumudini, Biprodas' sister, is caught between the two as she is married off to Madhusudan. She had risen in an observant and sheltered traditional home, as had all her female relations.

Others were uplifting: *Shesher Kobita*—translated twice as Last Poem and Farewell Song—is his most lyrical novel, with poems and rhythmic passages written by a poet protagonist. It contains elements of satire and postmodernism and has stock characters who gleefully attack the reputation of an old, outmoded, oppressively renowned poet who, incidentally, goes by a familiar name: 'Rabindranath Tagore'. Though his novels remain among the least-appreciated of his works, they have been given renewed attention via film adaptations by Ray and others: Chokher Bali and Ghare Baire are exemplary. In the first, Tagore inscribes Bengali society via its heroine: a rebellious widow who would live for herself alone. He pillories the custom of perpetual mourning on the part of widows, who were not allowed to remarry, who were consigned to seclusion and loneliness. Tagore wrote of it: 'I have always regretted the ending'.

> **Fun Fact:**
> Santiniketan's festivals like Basant Utsav were integral to its educational philosophy, teaching students the importance of cultural heritage, community, and the arts. These festivals unified students, teachers, and locals.

Poetry

Three-verse handwritten composition; each verse has original Bengali with English-language translation below: '*My fancies are fireflies: specks of living light twinkling in the dark. The same voice murmurs in these desultory lines, which is born in wayside pansies letting hasty glances pass by. The butterfly does not count years but moments, and therefore has enough time.*'

Part of a poem written by Tagore in Hungary, 1926.

Internationally, Gitanjali is Tagore's best-known collection of poetry, for which he was awarded the Nobel Prize in 1913. Tagore was the first person (excepting Roosevelt) outside Europe to get the Nobel Prize.

> **Fun Fact:**
> Sculpture Enthusiast: Despite being primarily known for his writing and painting, Tagore also sculpted, though few of his sculptures have survived.

Besides Gitanjali, other notable works include Manasi, Sonar Tori ('Golden Boat'), Balaka ('Wild Geese' — the title being a metaphor for migrating souls)

Tagore's poetic style, which proceeds from a lineage established by 15th- and 16th-century Vaishnava poets, ranges from classical formalism to the comic, visionary, and ecstatic. He was influenced by the atavistic mysticism of Vyasa and other rishi-authors of the Upanishads, the Bhakti-Sufi mystic Kabir, and Ramprasad Sen. Tagore's most innovative and mature poetry embodies his exposure to Bengali rural folk music, which included mystic Baul ballads such as those of the bard Lalon. These, rediscovered and repopularised by Tagore, resemble 19th-century Kartabhaja hymns that emphasise inward divinity and rebellion against bourgeois bhadralok religious and social orthodoxy. During his Shelaidaha years, his poems took on a lyrical voice of the moner manush, the Bauls' 'man within the heart' and Tagore's 'life force of his deep recesses', or meditating upon the jeevan devata—the demiurge or the 'living God within'. This figure connected with divinity through appeal to nature and the emotional interplay of human drama. Such tools saw use in his Bhānusiṃha poems chronicling the Radha-Krishna romance, which were repeatedly revised over the course of seventy years.

Later, with the development of new poetic ideas in Bengal — many originating from younger poets seeking to break with Tagore's style — Tagore absorbed new poetic concepts, which allowed him to further develop a unique identity. Examples of this include Africa and Camalia, which are among the better known of his latter poems.

Songs (Rabindra Sangeet)

Tagore was a prolific composer with around 2,230 songs to his credit. His songs are known as rabindrasangit ('Tagore Song'), which merges fluidly into his literature, most of which—poems or parts of novels, stories, or plays alike—were lyricised. Influenced by the thumri style of Hindustani music, they ran the entire gamut of human emotion, ranging from his early dirge-like Brahmo devotional hymns to quasi-erotic compositions. They emulated the tonal colour of classical ragas to varying extents. Some songs mimicked a given raga's melody and rhythm faithfully; others newly blended elements of different ragas. Yet about nine-tenths of his work was not bhanga gaan, the body of tunes revamped with 'fresh value' from select Western, Hindustani, Bengali folk and other regional flavours 'external' to Tagore's own ancestral culture.

> **Fun Fact:**
> Santiniketan maintains Tagore's essence, with outdoor classes and nature celebrations. Graduation ceremonies include chhatim leaves, symbolizing continuity. Tagore's vision of education in harmony with nature and promoting global exchange remains cherished in India.

In 1971, Amar Shonar Bangla became the national anthem of Bangladesh. It was written — ironically — to protest the 1905 Partition of Bengal along communal lines: cutting off the Muslim-majority East Bengal from Hindu-dominated West Bengal was to avert a regional bloodbath. Tagore saw the partition as a cunning plan to stop the independence movement, and he aimed to rekindle Bengali unity and tar communalism. Jana Gana Mana was written in shadhu-bhasha, a Sanskritised form of Bengali, and is the first of five stanzas of the Brahmo hymn Bharot Bhagyo Bidhata that Tagore composed. It was first sung in 1911 at a Calcutta session of the Indian National Congress and was adopted in 1950 by the Constituent Assembly of the Republic of India as its national anthem.

The Sri Lanka's National Anthem was inspired by his work.

For Bengalis, the songs' appeal, stemming from the combination of emotive strength and beauty described as surpassing even Tagore's poetry, was such that the Modern Review observed that 'there is in Bengal no cultured home where Rabindranath's songs are not sung or at least attempted to be sung... Even illiterate villagers sing his songs'. Tagore influenced sitar maestro Vilayat Khan and sarodiyas Buddhadev Dasgupta and Amjad Ali Khan.

Art works

At sixty, Tagore took up drawing and painting; successful exhibitions of his many works—which made a debut appearance in Paris upon encouragement by artists he met in the south of France —were held throughout Europe. He was likely red-green colour blind, resulting in works that exhibited strange colour schemes and off-beat aesthetics. Tagore was influenced numerous

Rabindranath Tagore (Portrait) by Chittaprosad
Credits: THL India, CC BY-SA 2.0 <https://creativecommons.org/licenses/by-sa/2.0>, via Wikimedia Commons

styles, including scrimshaw by the Malanggan people of northern New Ireland, Papua New Guinea, Haida carvings from the Pacific Northwest region of North America, and woodcuts by the German Max Pechstein. His artist's eye for his hand writing were revealed in the simple artistic and rhythmic leitmotifs embellishing the scribbles, cross-outs, and word layouts of his manuscripts. Some of Tagore's lyrics corresponded in a synesthetic sense with particular paintings.

Surrounded by several painters Rabindranath had always wanted to paint. Writing and music, playwriting and acting came to him

Rabindranath Tagore Statue in Dublin, Ireland
Credits: Satdeep Gill, CC BY-SA 4.0 <https://creativecommons.org/licenses/by-sa/4.0>, via Wikimedia Commons

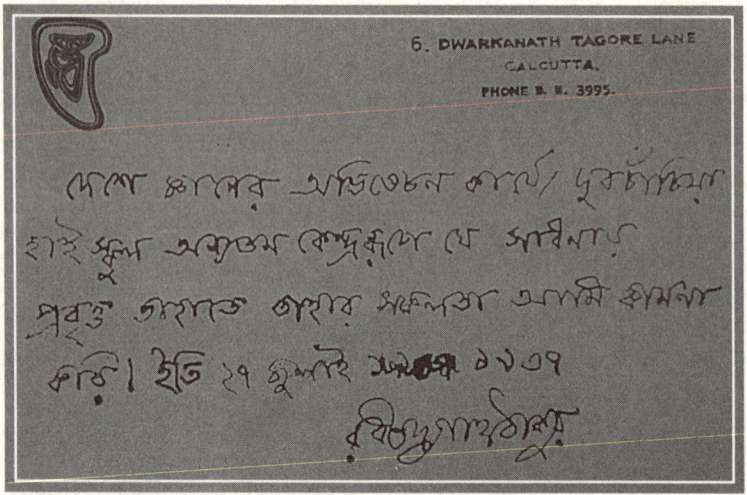

Calligraphy of Rabindranath Tagore made by Masum-al-Hasan Rocky
Credits: © Masum-al-hasan Rocky / Wikimedia Commons / "Rabindronath Tagore at dupchanchia model high school"

naturally and almost without training, as it did to several others in his family, and in even greater measure. But painting eluded him. Yet he tried repeatedly to master the art and there are several references to this in his early letters and reminiscence. In 1900 for instance, when he was nearing forty and already a celebrated writer, he wrote to Jagadishchandra Bose, 'You will be surprised to hear that I am sitting with a sketchbook drawing. Needless to say, the pictures are not intended for any salon in Paris, they cause me not the least suspicion that the national gallery of any country will suddenly decide to raise taxes to acquire them. But, just as a mother lavishes most affection on her ugliest son, so I feel secretly drawn to the very skill that comes to me least easily.' He also realized that he was using the eraser more than the pencil, and dissatisfied with the results he finally withdrew, deciding it was not for him to become a painter.

Tagore also had an artist's eye for his handwriting, embellishing his manuscripts' cross-outs and word layouts with simple artistic leitmotifs.

4

Tagore's political views, educational philosophy, and legacy

Both Nehru and Tagore were instrumental in shaping modern India, sharing a deep commitment to the country's progress and the upliftment of its people, albeit in different spheres. Tagore's emphasis on education and culture complemented Nehru's focus on political and economic development, and their shared values of secularism, humanism, and a vision for an inclusive India accentuated Tagore's influence on Nehru. Nehru admired Tagore's literary genius and progressive views on education and society, and their correspondence and interactions often revolved around discussions on India's future and the challenges it faced.

Jawaharlal Nehru and Rabindranath Tagore
Credits: Royroydeb, Public domain, via Wikimedia Commons

Photo of a formal function, an aged bald man and old woman in simple white robes are seated side-by-side with legs folded on a rug-strewn dais; the man looks at a bearded and garlanded old man seated on another dais at left. In the foreground, various ceremonial objects are arrayed; in the background, dozens of other people observe.

Tagore opposed imperialism and supported Indian nationalists, and these views were first revealed in Manast, which was mostly composed in his twenties. Evidence produced during the Hindu–German Conspiracy Trial and latter accounts affirm his awareness of the Ghadarites, and stated that he sought the support of Japanese Prime Minister Terauchi Masatake and former Premier Okuma Shigenobu. Yet he lampooned the Swadeshi movement; he rebuked it in The Cult of the Charkha, an acrid 1925 essay. He urged the masses to avoid victimology and instead seek self-help and education, and he saw the presence of British administration as a 'political symptom of our social disease'. He maintained that, even for those at the extremes of poverty, 'there can be no question of blind revolution'; preferable to it was a 'steady and purposeful education'.

So I repeat we never can have a true view of man unless we have a love for him. Civilization must be judged and prized, not by the amount of power it has developed, but by how much it has evolved and given expression to, by its laws and institutions, the love of humanity.

Such views enraged many. He escaped assassination—and only narrowly—by Indian expatriates during his stay in a San Francisco hotel in late 1916; the plot failed when his would-be assassins fell into argument. Tagore wrote songs lionizing the Indian independence movement. Two of Tagore's more politically charged compositions, 'Chitto Jetha Bhayshunyo' ('Where the Mind is Without Fear') and 'Ekla Chalo Re' ('If They Answer Not to Thy Call, Walk Alone'), gained mass appeal, with the latter favoured by Gandhi. Though somewhat critical of Gandhian activism, Tagore was key in resolving a Gandhi–Ambedkar dispute involving separate electorates for untouchables, thereby mooting at least one of Gandhi's fasts 'unto death'.

Repudiation of knighthood

Tagore renounced his knighthood in response to the Jallianwala Bagh massacre in 1919. In the repudiation letter to the Viceroy, Lord Chelmsford, he wrote

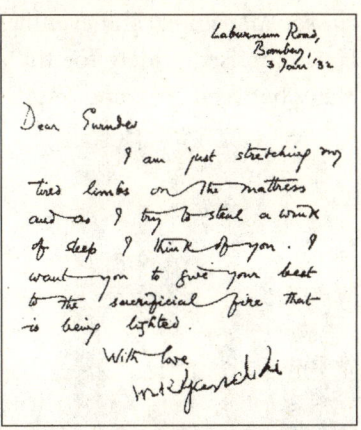

Gandhi to Tagore 1932
Credits: Mohandas K. Gandhi, Public domain, via Wikimedia Commons

The time has come when badges of honour make our shame glaring in the incongruous context of humiliation, and I for my part, wish to stand, shorn, of all special distinctions, by the side of those of my countrymen who, for their so called insignificance, are liable to suffer degradation not fit for human beings.

Shantiniketan and Visva-Bharati

Tagore despised rote classroom schooling: in 'The Parrot's Training', a bird is caged and force-fed textbook pages—to death. Tagore, visiting Santa Barbara in 1917, conceived a new type of university: he sought to 'make Shantiniketan the connecting thread between India and the world and a world center for the study of humanity somewhere beyond the limits of nation and geography.' The school, which he named Visva-Bharati, had its foundation stone laid on 24 December 1918 and was inaugurated precisely three years later. Tagore employed a brahmacharya system: gurus gave pupils personal guidance—emotional, intellectual, and spiritual. Teaching was often done under trees. He staffed the school, he contributed his Nobel Prize monies, and his duties as steward-mentor at Shantiniketan kept him busy: mornings he taught classes; afternoons and evenings he wrote the students' textbooks. He fundraised widely for the school in Europe and the United States between 1919 and 1921.

Rabindranath Tagore surrounded by students at Shantiniketan, 1925

Theft of Nobel Prize

On 25 March 2004, Tagore's Nobel Prize was stolen from the safety vault of the Visva-Bharati University, along with several other of his belongings. On 7 December 2004, the Swedish Academy decided to present two replicas of Tagore's Nobel Prize, one made of gold and the other made of bronze, to the Visva-Bharati University. It inspired the fictional film Nobel Chor.

5

Selected Quotes of Rabindranath Tagore

- A dewdrop is a perfect integrity that has no filial memory of its parentage.
- A mind all logic is like a knife all blade. It makes the hand bleed that uses it.

According to the true Indian view, our consciousness of the world, merely as the sum total of things that exist, and as governed by laws, is imperfect. But it is perfect when our consciousness realizes all things as spiritually one with it, and therefore capable of giving us joy. For us the highest purpose of this world is not merely living in it, knowing it and making use of it, but realizing our own selves in it through expansion of sympathy; not alienating ourselves from it and dominating it, but comprehending and uniting it with ourselves in perfect union.

All men have poetry in their hearts, and it is necessary for them, as much as possible, to express their feelings. For this they must have a medium, moving and pliant, which can refreshingly become their own, age after age. All great languages undergo change. Those languages which resist the spirit of change are doomed and will never produce great harvests of thought and literature. When forms become fixed, the spirit either weakly accepts its imprisonment or rebels. All revolutions consists of the 'within' fighting against invasion from 'without'... All great human movements are related to some great idea.

Beauty is in the ideal of perfect harmony which is in the universal being; truth the perfect comprehension of the universal mind. We individuals approach it through our own mistakes and blunders, through our accumulated experience, through our illumined consciousness – how, otherwise, can we know truth?

Children are living beings – more living than grown-up people who have built shells of habit around themselves. Therefore it is absolutely necessary for their mental health and development that they should not have mere schools for their lessons, but a world whose guiding spirit is personal love.

> **Fun Fact:**
> Santiniketan's vibrant festivals and unique architecture, combined with Visva Bharati University's artistic freedom, create a distinct educational experience. Notable alumni include Amartya Sen, Satyajit Ray, and international figures like Indonesian painter Affandi.

- Death is not extinguishing the light; it is putting out the lamp because the dawn has come.
- Do not say, 'It is morning,' and dismiss it with a name of yesterday. See it for the first time as a new-born child that has no name.

> **Fun Fact:**
> Phobia of Lawns: Tagore had a strange aversion to manicured lawns, preferring wild, untamed gardens which he felt were more natural.

For the current of our spiritual life creeds, rituals and channels that may thwart or help, according to their fixity or openness. When a symbol or spiritual idea becomes rigidly elaborate in its construction, it supplants the idea which it should support.

Gross utility kills beauty. We now have all over the world huge production of things, huge organizations, huge administrations of empire – all obstructing the path of life. Civilization is waiting for a great consummation, for an expression of its soul in beauty. This must be your contribution to the world.

- He who wants to do good knocks at the gate; he who loves finds the gate open.

- I have spent my days stringing and unstringing my instrument while the song I came to sing remains unsung.
- I slept and dreamt that life was joy. I awoke and saw that life was service. I acted and behold, service was joy.
- If you shut your door to all errors truth will be shut out.

In love all the contradiction of existence merge themselves and are lost. Only in love are unity and duality not at variance. Love must be one and two at the same time. Only love is motion and rest in one. Our heart ever changes its place till it finds love, and then it has its rest... Bondage and liberation are not antagonistic in love. for love is most free and at the same time most bound.

> **Fun Fact:**
> The institution's commitment to rural reconstruction uplifted the local Santhal community, focusing on vocational training and promoting cottage industries. This rural development mission extended to Sriniketan, promoting sustainable agricultural practices.

In our desire for eternal life we pray for an eternity of our habit and comfort, forgetting that immortality is in repeatedly transcending the definite forms of life in order to pursue the infinite truth of life.

In the dualism of death and life there is a harmony. We know that the life of a soul, which is finite in its expression and infinite in its principle, must go through the portals of death in its journey to realise the infinite. It is death which is monistic, it has no life in it. But life is dualistic; it has an appearance as well as truth; and death is that appearance, that maya, which is an inseparable companion to life.

> **Fun Fact:**
> Tagore's internationalism brought global scholars and artists to Visva Bharati University, fostering cultural exchange. Reviving Indian arts and promoting diverse cultural expressions ensured Santiniketan's status as a cultural hub.

Rabindranath Tagore With Sir Maurice Gwyer and Dr. S. Radhakrishnan at Sinha Sadan after the Oxford University Convocation on 7 August 1940. Sir Maurice Gwyer, Founder of Miranda House, University of Delhi.

In the night we stumble over things and become acutely conscious of their separateness, but the day reveals the unity which embraces them. And the man whose inner vision is bathed in consciousness at once realizes the spiritual unity which reigns over all racial differences, and his mind no longer stumbles over individual facts, accepting them as final. He realizes that peace is an inner harmony and not an outer adjustment, that beauty carries the assurance of our relationship to reality, which waits for its perfection in the response of our love.

- Leave out my name from the gift if it be a burden, but keep my song.
- Let the dead have the immortality of fame, but the living the immortality of love.
- Let us not pray to be sheltered from dangers but to be fearless when facing them.
- Life is given to us, we earn it by giving it.

Love gives beauty to everything it touches. Not greed and utility; they produce offices, but not dwelling houses. To be able to love material things, to clothe them with tender grace,

> **Fun Fact:**
> Voice Recordings: Tagore's voice was recorded in 1921 on a wax cylinder, one of the earliest recordings of an Indian's voice.

and yet not be attached to them, this is a great service. Providence expects that we should make this world our own, and not live in it as though it were a rented tenement. We can only make it our own through some service, and that service is to lend it love and beauty from our soul. Your own experience shows you the difference between the beautiful, the tender, the hospitable, and the mechanically neat and monotonously useful.

> **Fun Fact:**
> Amulet Incident: As a child, Tagore's father gave him an amulet to wear for protection, which he promptly lost while playing.

- Love is an endless mystery, for it has nothing else to explain it.
- Love is not a mere impulse, it must contain truth, which is law.
- Love is the only reality and it is not a mere sentiment. It is the ultimate truth that lies at the heart of creation.
- Man is cry is to reach his fullest expression.
- Men are cruel, but Man is kind.
- Music fills the infinite between two souls. This has been muffled by the mist of our daily habits.
- Never be afraid of the moments – thus sings the voice of the ever-lasting.

Objects of knowledge maintain an infinite distance from us who are the knowers. For knowledge is not union. Therefore the further world of freedom awaits us there where we reach truth, not through feeling it by senses or knowing it by reason, but through union of perfect sympathy.

Obstacles are necessary companions to expression, and we know that the positive element in language is not in its obstructiveness. Exclusively

> **Fun Fact:**
> Santiniketan's architecture blends with nature, reflecting Tagore's aesthetic philosophy. The Uttarayan Complex's unique houses and artistic decorations embody this harmony, contributing to Santiniketan's rich cultural environment.

> **Fun Fact:**
> Santiniketan's architecture, with mud buildings and frescoes, blended seamlessly with the natural environment, reflecting Tagore's belief in man-nature harmony. The Uttarayan Complex, where Tagore lived, stands as a testament to this philosophy.

viewed from the side of the obstacle, nature appears inimical to the idea of morality. But if that were absolutely true, moral life could never come to exists. Life, moral or physical, is not a completed fact, but a continual process, depending for its movement upon two contrary forces, the force of resistance and that of expression. Dividing these forces into two mutually opposing principles does not help us, for the truth dwells not in the opposition but in its continual reconciliation.

- Our creation is the modification of relationship.
- Praise shames me, for I secretly beg for it.

Religion is not a fractional thing that can be doled out in fixed weekly or daily measures as one among various subjects in the school syllabus. It is the truth of our complete being, the consciousness of our personal relationship with the infinite; it is the true center of gravity of our life. This we can attain during our childhood by daily living in a place where the truth of the spiritual world is not obscured by a crowd of necessities assuming artificial importance; where life is simple, surrounded by fullness of leisure, by ample space and pure air and profound peace of nature; and where men live with a perfect faith in the eternal life before them.

Religion, like poetry, is not a mere idea, it is expression. The self-expression of God is in the endless variety of creation; and our attitude toward the Infinite

> **Fun Fact:**
> Rabindra Bhavan Museum offers a glimpse into Tagore's life, housing manuscripts, artifacts, and his Nobel Prize. It inspires visitors and underscores Santiniketan's illustrious heritage, showcasing Tagore's multifaceted genius.

Being must also in its expression have a variety of individuality ceaseless and unending. Those sects which jealously build their boundaries with too rigid creeds excluding all spontaneous movement of the living spirit may hoard their theology but they kill religion.

Science urges us to occupy by our mind the immensity of the knowable world; our spiritual teacher enjoins us to comprehend by our soul the infinite spirit which is in the depth of the moving and changing facts of the world; the urging of our artistic nature is to realize the manifestation of personality in the world of appearance, the reality of existence which is in harmony with the real within us. Where this harmony is not deeply felt, there we are aliens and perpetually homesick. For man by nature is an artist; he never receives passively and accurately in his mind a physical representation of things around him.

> **Fun Fact:**
> Cultural Critic: Tagore was a sharp critic of Western materialism and capitalism, which he often addressed in his essays and speeches

- That I exist is a perpetual surprise which is life.

The best of us still have our aspirations for the supreme goals of life, which is so often mocked by prosperous people who now control the world. We still believe that the world has a deeper meaning than what is apparent, and that therein the human soul finds its ultimate harmony and peace. We still know that only in spiritual wealth does civilization attain its end, not in a prolific production of materials, and not in the competition of intemperate power with power.

The child learns so easily because he has a natural gift, but adults, because they are tyrants, ignore natural gifts and say that children must learn

> **Fun Fact:**
> Lost in Translation: Tagore often re-translated his own works multiple times to better capture the essence, leading to several versions of the same piece.

through the same process that they learned by. We insist upon forced mental feeding and our lessons become a form of torture. This is one of man ís most cruel and wasteful mistakes.

The current of the world has its boundaries, otherwise it could have no existence, but its purpose is not shown in the boundaries which restrain it, but in its movement, which is toward perfection. The wonder is not that there should be obstacles and sufferings in this world, but that there should be law and order, beauty and joy, goodness and love.

Stamp of India - 2011 - 150th Birth Anniversary
Credits: Post of India

The emancipation of our physical nature is in attaining health, of our social being in attaining goodness, and of our self in attaining love.

The picture of a flower in a botanical book is information; its mission ends with our knowledge. But in pure art it is a personal communication. And therefore until it finds its harmony in the depth of our personality it misses the mark. We can treat existence solely as a textbook furnishing us lessons, and we shall not be disappointed, but we know that there its mission does not end. For in our joy in it, which is an end in itself, we feel that it is a communication, the final response of our knowing but the response of our being.

Fun Fact:
Silent Film Appearance: Tagore made a cameo in the silent film "Natir Puja," which he also directed.

• The potentiality of perfection outweighs actual contradictions… Existence in itself is here to prove that it cannot be an evil.

The progress of our soul is like a perfect poem. It has an infinite idea which once realised makes all movements full of meaning and joy. But if we detach its movements from that ultimate idea, if we do not see the infinite rest and only see the infinite motion, then existence appears to us a monstrous evil., impetuously rushing towards an unending aimlessness.

- The significance which is in unity is an eternal wonder.
- The water in a vessel is sparkling; the water in the sea is dark. The small truth has words which are clear; the great truth has great silence.

> **Fun Fact:**
> Santiniketan's ethos of inclusive, holistic education remains relevant today. Its commitment to traditional crafts, environmental sustainability, and cultural diversity preserves Tagore's visionary educational model.

There are men whose idea of life is tactic, who long for its continuation after death only because of their wish for permanence and not perfection; they love to imagine that the things to which they are accustomed will persist for ever. They completely identify themselves in their minds with their fixed surroundings and with whatever they have gathered, and to have to leave these is death for them. They forget that the true meaning of living is outliving, it is ever growing out of itself.

There is a point where in the mystery of existence contradictions meet; where movement is not all movement and stillness is not all stillness; where the idea and the form, the within and the without, are united; where infinite becomes finite, yet not losing its infinity. If this meeting is dissolved, then things become unreal.

> **Fun Fact:**
> Early Innovator: At 11, Tagore wrote his first short story and sent it anonymously to a family journal, which they published without knowing it was his.

Things are distinct not in their essence but in their appearance; in other words, in their relation to one to whom they appear. This is art, the truth of which is not in substance or logic, but in expression. Abstract truth may belong to science and metaphysics, but the world of reality belongs to art.

Things in which we do not take joy are either a burden upon our minds to be got rid of at any cost; or they are useful, and therefore in temporary and partial relation to us, becoming burdensome when

> **Fun Fact:**
> The Rabindra Bhavan Museum, designed by Tagore's son, showcases Tagore's manuscripts, photographs, and personal artifacts, including his Nobel Prize medallion, offering insights into his multifaceted genius and Santiniketan's illustrious heritage.

their utility is lost; or they are like wandering vagabonds, loitering for a moment on the outskirts of our recognition, and then passing on. A thing is only completely our own when it is a thing of joy to us.

This is the ultimate end of man, to find the One which is in him; which is his truth, which is his soul; the key with which he opens the gate of the spiritual life, the heavenly kingdom.

Those institutions which are static in their nature raise walls of division; this is why, in the history of religions, priesthood has always maintained dissensions and hindered the freedom of man. But the principle of life unites, it deals with the varied, and seeks unity.

To understand anything is to find in it something which is our own, and it is the discovery of ourselves outside us which makes us glad. This relation of understanding is partial, but the relation of love is complete. In love the sense of difference is obliterated and the human soul fulfills its purpose in perfection, transcending the limits of itself and reaching across the threshold of the infinite. Therefore love is the highest bliss that man can attain to, for through it alone he truly knows that he is more than himself, and that he is at one with the All.

> **Fun Fact:**
> Tagore's transformative vision at Santiniketan emphasizes free, unbounded knowledge, making it a living embodiment of his ideals. This educational philosophy continues to inspire, guiding Santiniketan as a unique, enduring institution.

Want of love is a degree of callousness; for love is the perfection of consciousness. We do not love because we do not comprehend, or rather we do not comprehend because we do not love. For love is the ultimate meaning of everything around us. It is not a mere sentiment; it is truth; it is the joy that is at the root of all creation.

We can look upon a road from two different points of view. One regards it as dividing us from the object of desire; in that case we count every step of our journey over it as something attained by force in the face of obstruction. The other sees it as the road which leads us to our destination; and as such is part of our goal. It is already the beginning of our attainment, and by journeying over it we can only gain that which in itself it offers to us.

We can make truth ours by actively modulating its inter-relations. This is the work of art; for reality is not based in the substance of things but in the principle of relationship. Truth is the infinite pursued by metaphysics; fact is the infinite pursued by science, while reality is the definition of the infinite which relates truth to the person. Reality is human; it is what we are conscious of, by which we are affected, that which we express.

- We come nearest to the great when we are great in humility.

Whenever our life is stirred by truth, it expresses energy and comes to be filled, as it were, with a creative ardor. This consciousness of the creative urge is evidence of the force of truth on our mind.

All men have poetry in their hearts, and it is necessary for them, as much as possible, to express their feelings. For this they must

> **Fun Fact:**
> Nobel Confusion: Tagore initially didn't know he'd won the Nobel Prize in Literature in 1913 because the notification letter was sent to a wrong address.

> **Fun Fact:**
> Rabindra Bhavan Museum, designed by Tagore's son, showcases manuscripts, photos, and Tagore's Nobel Prize. Key sites include Santiniketan Griha and Upasana Griha. Nearby Sriniketan focuses on rural industries like pottery and leatherwork.

> **Fun Fact:**
> Walt Whitman Influence: Tagore was greatly influenced by Walt Whitman's "Leaves of Grass," which he read during his travels in the U.S.

have a medium, moving and pliant, which can refreshingly become their own, age after age. All great languages undergo change. Those languages which resist the spirit of change are doomed and will never produce great harvests of thought and literature. When forms become fixed, the spirit either weakly accepts its imprisonment or rebels. All revolutions consists of the 'within' fighting against invasion from 'without'… All great human movements are related to some great idea.

Beauty is in the ideal of perfect harmony which is in the universal being; truth the perfect comprehension of the universal mind. We individuals approach it through our own mistakes and blunders, through our accumulated experience, through our illumined consciousness – how, otherwise, can we know truth?

- Death belongs to life as birth does. The walk is in the raising of the foot as in the laying of it down.

> **Fun Fact:**
> Santiniketan's open studios and emphasis on artistic freedom nurture new generations of thinkers, artists, and leaders. Its alumni, including Amartya Sen and Satyajit Ray, have made significant contributions in various fields, carrying forward Tagore's legacy.

God finds himself by creating.

- He is neither manifest nor hidden, He is neither revealed nor unrevealed: there are no words to tell that which He is. He is without form, without quality, without decay.
- He who wants to do good knocks at the gate; he who loves finds the gate open.

I believe that there is an ideal hovering over the earth, an ideal of that Paradise which is not the mere outcome of imagination, but the ultimate reality towards which all things are moving.

I believe that this vision of Paradise is to be seen in the sunlight, and the green of the earth, in the flowing streams, in the beauty of springtime and the repose of a winter morning. Everywhere in this earth the spirit of Paradise is awake and sending forth its voice

If anger be the basis of our political activities, the excitement tends to become an end in itself, at the expense of the object to be achieved. side issues then assume an exaggerated importance, and all gravity of thought and action is lost; such excitement is not an exercise of strength, but a display of weakness.

- If I say that He is within me, the universe is ashamed; if I say that He is without me, it is falsehood.

> **Fun Fact:**
> Synesthesia: Tagore is believed to have had synesthesia, a condition where one sense is simultaneously perceived by one or more additional senses.

If life is journey be endless where is its goal? The answer is, it is everywhere. We are in a palace which has no end, but which we have reached. By exploring it and extending our relationship with it we are ever making it more and more our own. The infant is born in the same universe where lives the adult of ripe mind. But its position is not like a schoolboy who has yet to learn his alphabet, finding himself in a college class. The infant has it own joy of life because the world is not a mere road, but a home, of which it will have more and more as it grows up in wisdom. With our road that gain is at every step, for it is the road and the home in one; it leads us on yet gives us shelter.

In love, at one of its poles you find the personal, at the other the impersonal. At one you have the positive assertion – Here I am; at the other the equally strong denial – I am not. Without this ego what is

> **Fun Fact:**
> Tagore supported diverse art forms, inviting global artists and scholars to Santiniketan. He revived folk dances and introduced new ones, celebrating culture through festivals like Basant Utsav and Nandan Mela, promoting Bengal's traditional arts and crafts.

love? And again, with only this ego how can love be possible?

In the dualism of death and life there is a harmony. Life of a soul, which is finite in its expression and infinite in its principle, must go through the portals of death in its journey to realise the infinite. It is death which is monistic, it has no life in it. But life is dualistic; it has an appearance as well as truth; and death is that appearance, that maya, which is an inseparable companion to life.

In the night we stumble over things and become acutely conscious of their separateness, but the day reveals the unity which embraces them. And the man whose inner vision is bathed in consciousness at once realizes the spiritual unity which reigns over all racial differences, and his mind no longer stumbles over individual facts, accepting them as final. He realizes that peace is an inner harmony and not an outer adjustment, that beauty carries the assurance of our relationship to reality, which waits for its perfection in the response of our love.

> **Fun Fact:**
> Futuristic Views: Tagore predicted the rise of robotics and artificial intelligence in his short story "The Victory," where a mechanical man is used in warfare

It is our desires that limit the scope of our self-realisation, hinder our extension of consciousness, and give rise to sin, which is the innermost barrier that keeps us apart from our God, setting up disunion and arrogance of exclusiveness. For sin is not one mere action, but it is an attitude of life which takes for granted that our goal is finite, that our self is the ultimate truth, and that we are not all essentially one but exist each for his own separate individual existence.

6

Interview of Tagore with Einstein: Meeting of two great minds

Tagore and Einstein met through a common friend, Dr. Mendel. Tagore visited Einstein at his residence at Kaputh in the suburbs of Berlin on July 14, 1930, and Einstein returned the call and visited Tagore at the Mendel home. The July 14 conversation is reproduced here:

TAGORE: I was discussing with Dr. Mendel today the new mathematical discoveries which tell us that in the realm of infinitesimal atoms chance has its play; the drama of existence is not absolutely predestined in character.

> **Fun Fact:**
> Meteorite Composition: Tagore composed a poem inspired by a meteorite that fell in Shantiniketan, which he later gifted to Einstein.

EINSTEIN: The facts that make science tend toward this view do not say good-bye to causality.

EINSTEIN: One tries to understand in the higher plane how the order is. The order is there, where the big elements combine and guide existence, but in the minute elements this order is not perceptible.

TAGORE: Thus duality is in the depths of existence, the contradiction of free impulse and the directive will which works upon it and evolves an orderly scheme of things.

EINSTEIN: Modern physics would not say they are contradictory. Clouds look as one from a distance, but if you see them nearby, they show themselves as disorderly drops of water.

TAGORE: I find a parallel in human psychology. Our passions and desires are unruly, but our character subdues these elements into a harmonious whole. Does something similar to this happen in the physical world? Are the elements rebellious, dynamic with individual impulse? And is there a principle in the physical world which dominates them and puts them into an orderly organization?

EINSTEIN: Even the elements are not without statistical order; elements of radium will always maintain their specific order, now and ever onward, just as they have done all along. There is, then, a statistical order in the elements.

TAGORE: Otherwise, the drama of existence would be too desultory. It is the constant harmony of chance and determination which makes it eternally new and living.

EINSTEIN: I believe that whatever we do or live for has its causality; it is good, however, that we cannot see through to it.

TAGORE: There is in human affairs an element of elasticity also, some freedom within a small range which is for the expression of our personality. It is like the musical system in India, which is not

Einstein and Tagore Berlin, 14 July 1930
Credits: Martin Vos, Public domain, via Wikimedia Commons

so rigidly fixed as western music. Our composers give a certain definite outline, a system of melody and rhythmic arrangement, and within a certain limit the player can improvise upon it. He must be one with the law of that particular melody, and then he can give spontaneous expression to his musical feeling within the prescribed regulation. We praise the composer for his genius in creating a foundation along with a superstructure of melodies, but we expect from the player his own skill in the creation of variations of melodic flourish and ornamentation. In creation we follow the central law of existence, but if we do not cut ourselves adrift from it, we can have sufficient freedom within the limits of our personality for the fullest self-expression.

EINSTEIN: That is possible only when there is a strong artistic tradition in music to guide the people's mind. In Europe, music has come too far away from popular art and popular feeling and has become something like a secret art with conventions and traditions of its own.

TAGORE: You have to be absolutely obedient to this too complicated music. In India, the measure of a singer's freedom is in his own creative personality. He can sing the composer's song as his own, if he has the power creatively to assert himself in his interpretation of the general law of the melody which he is given to interpret.

EINSTEIN: It requires a very high standard of art to realize fully the great idea in the original music, so that one can make variations upon it. In our country, the variations are often prescribed.

> **Fun Fact:**
> Invented Writing System: Tagore created his own phonetic alphabet to simplify Bengali script, though it never gained widespread adoption.

TAGORE: If in our conduct we can follow the law of goodness, we can have real liberty of self-expression. The principle of conduct is there, but the character which makes it true and individual is our own creation. In our music there is a duality of freedom and prescribed order.

EINSTEIN: Are the words of a song also free? I mean to say, is the singer at liberty to add his own words to the song which he is singing?

TAGORE: Yes. In Bengal we have a kind of song-kirtan, we call it-which gives freedom to the singer to introduce parenthetical comments, phrases not in the original song. This occasions great enthusiasm, since the audience is constantly thrilled by some beautiful, spontaneous sentiment added by the singer.

EINSTEIN: Is the metrical form quite severe?

TAGORE: Yes, quite. You cannot exceed the limits of versification; the singer in all his variations must keep the rhythm and the time, which is fixed. In European music you have a comparative liberty with time, but not with melody.

EINSTEIN: Can the Indian music be sung without words? Can one understand a song without words?

TAGORE: Yes, we have songs with unmeaning words, sounds which just help to act as carriers of the notes. In North India, music is an independent art, not the interpretation of words and thoughts, as in Bengal. The music is very intricate and subtle and is a complete world of melody by itself.

EINSTEIN: Is it not polyphonic?

TAGORE: Instruments are used, not for harmony, but for keeping time and adding to the volume and depth. Has melody suffered in your music by the imposition of harmony?

EINSTEIN: Sometimes it does suffer very much. Sometimes the harmony swallows up the melody altogether.

TAGORE: Melody and harmony are like lines and colors in pictures. A simple linear picture may be completely beautiful; the introduction of color may make it vague and insignificant. Yet color may, by combination with lines, create great pictures, so long as it does not smother and destroy their value.

EINSTEIN: It is a beautiful comparison; line is also much older than color. It seems that your melody is much richer in structure than ours. Japanese music also seems to be so.

Rabindranath Tagore in Japan, 1916, with Yokoyama Taikan (far right)
Credits: Asahigraph, 1951 New Year's Issue, Public domain, via Wikimedia Commons

TAGORE: It is difficult to analyze the effect of eastern and western music on our minds. I am deeply moved by the western music; I feel that it is great, that it is vast in its structure and grand in its composition. Our own music touches me more deeply by its fundamental lyrical appeal. European music is epic in character; it has a broad background and is Gothic in its structure.

EINSTEIN: This is a question we Europeans cannot properly answer, we are so used to our own music. We want to know whether our own music is a conventional or a fundamental human feeling, whether to feel consonance and dissonance is natural, or a convention which we accept.

TAGORE: Somehow the piano confounds me. The violin pleases me much more.

EINSTEIN: It would be interesting to study the effects of European music on an Indian who had never heard it when he was young.

TAGORE: Once I asked an English musician to analyze for me some classical music, and explain to me what elements make for the beauty of the piece.

EINSTEIN: The difficulty is that the really good music, whether of the East or of the West, cannot be analyzed.

TAGORE: Yes, and what deeply affects the hearer is beyond himself.

Rabindranath Tagore with family. Left to right: youngest daughter Mira Devi, eldest son Rathindranath Tagore, Rabindranath Tagore, wife of Rathindranath Protima Devi, eldest daughter of R. Tagore Madhurilata Devi

Fun Fact:

Santiniketan pioneered humane, environmentally friendly education, emphasizing holistic development and co-education. Tagore won the Nobel Prize in 1913 for Gitanjali, boosting Santiniketan's prestige. In 1921, it became Visva Bharati University, a global educational institution.

EINSTEIN: The same uncertainty will always be there about everything fundamental in our experience, in our reaction to art, whether in Europe or in Asia. Even the red flower I see before me on your table may not be the same to you and me.

TAGORE: And yet there is always going on the process of reconciliation between them, the individual taste conforming to the universal standard.

7

Tagore and Cinema

In the late 1920s, Tagore's passion for cinema took a tangible form. His first significant brush with motion pictures occurred in 1923 with "Sriniketan," a film based on his own philosophical ideas. However, it was in 1929 that Tagore's directorial vision truly materialized. Dominion Films Limited decided to create a film based on Tagore's play "Tapati." Filming took place in Santiniketan, and Tagore not only directed but also starred in the movie, a testament to his multifaceted talent.

The film "Notir Puja," which adapts Tagore's poem "Pujarini," embodies his pioneering spirit. The poem, written in 1906, tells a powerful story set 2500 years ago about Shrimati, a court dancer who defies the anti-Buddhist king Ajatashatru by worshipping Buddha, leading to her execution. Tagore's daughter-in-law, Pratima Debi, first adapted this poignant narrative, highlighting themes of faith, defiance, and sacrifice, into a play in 1927 for his seventieth birthday celebrations. The play was well-received, and its success paved the way for its cinematic adaptation.

Birendra Nath Sircar, a prominent film producer and owner of the New Empire Theatre, produced the cinematic version of "Notir Puja". The New Empire, a prestigious venue in Kolkata, became the setting for this groundbreaking project. Despite the economic challenges faced by Santiniketan at the time, Tagore accepted Sircar's proposal, agreeing to direct the film with the promise of sharing half of the proceeds from ticket sales.

Tagore's direction of "Notir Puja" was notable for its innovative use of one-shot cinematography, a technique that captured entire scenes in a single, continuous take. This method was revolutionary for its time and drew the admiration of international filmmakers, including Russian director Sergei Solovyov, who employed it in his adaptation of Chekhov's "Three Sisters."

Despite the lack of modern comforts like air conditioning, which made the summer shoot challenging, the cast and crew persevered, driven by Tagore's vision. During the shoot, a straw house under a mango tree served as Tagore's resting place, earning him the humorous nickname "Second Santiniketan."

When "Notir Puja" premiered on March 22, 1932, at Chitra Cinema Hall, Tagore himself was present. The film, though not a commercial success, was a cultural milestone. It stood out for its artistic and technical achievements, as well as its progressive social messages. Tagore's portrayal of Upali, a Buddhist monk, alongside performances by women from elite backgrounds, underscored the film's unique approach to storytelling and societal commentary.

The film's legacy extends far beyond its immediate impact. Tagore's innovative cinematography techniques revolutionised the art of filmmaking, influencing directors and cinematographers worldwide. His inclusive casting choices and steadfast advocacy for women's participation in the arts were groundbreaking, paving the way for future generations. "Notir Puja" stands as a testament to Tagore's enduring influence and his ability to inspire societal change through creativity.

One of the most significant aspects of "Notir Puja" was its progressive stance on women's involvement in the arts. At a time when societal norms severely restricted women's roles in public and professional life, Tagore boldly cast his female students from aristocratic families in the film. This decision not only challenged societal conventions but also promoted a silent yet powerful feminist movement. The film's promotional materials even encouraged men to bring their wives to the theatre, a subtle push towards greater gender inclusivity in public spaces.

Moreover, Tagore's deep understanding of the socio-political context of his time marked his approach to filmmaking. By casting women in prominent roles and giving them a platform to express themselves artistically, he directly confronted and questioned the patriarchal structures of society. This act of defiance against the traditional roles prescribed to women was not just a statement of artistic freedom but also a call for social reform.

In reflecting on Rabindranath Tagore's contributions to cinema, we celebrate a visionary who continually pushed the boundaries of artistic expression. "Notir Puja" highlighted the cultural richness and diversity of Bengal, bringing its traditional music, dance, and storytelling techniques to a broader audience. Tagore's work in cinema, though less renowned than his literary achievements, is a vital part of his legacy, illustrating the breadth and depth of his artistic genius.

Through his films, as well as his writings, Tagore left an indelible mark on the world, reminding us of the power of creativity to drive progress and foster understanding.

Rabindranath Tagore in modern times

Rabindranath Tagore's vast body of work continues to influence various fields, prompting new interpretations and applications. This extended exploration aims to delve deeper into the nuances of his contributions and their relevance today.

1. Literary and Cultural Studies

Tagore's Narrative Techniques
- Tagore's mastery of weaving intricate narrative structures and character development offers rich material for literary analysis. His stories often explore the human condition, relationships, and the social environment with a nuanced understanding that transcends cultural boundaries.
- Modern literary critics analyse Tagore's work through lenses like postcolonialism, examining how he addresses themes of identity, power, and resistance within the colonial context.

Gender Studies and Feminism
- Tagore's portrayal of women and his exploration of gender dynamics are complex and ahead of their time. Characters like Charulata in "Nastanirh" (The Broken Nest) and Binodini in "Chokher Bali" (A Grain of Sand) challenge traditional gender roles and societal expectations.
- Feminist scholars find Tagore's works fertile ground for examining early expressions of women's autonomy and the critique of patriarchal structures.

2. Educational Philosophy
Shantiniketan's Pedagogical Innovations
- Tagore's educational philosophy at Shantiniketan emphasised creativity, freedom, and a close relationship with nature. This approach contrasts with conventional educational systems, advocating for the holistic development of individuals.
- Contemporary educators draw inspiration from Tagore's methods, integrating arts, culture, and environmental awareness into curriculums to foster well-rounded growth.

Lifelong Learning and Social Reform
- Tagore believed in education as a lifelong process and a means of social reform. His initiatives for rural education and development aimed to empower marginalised communities through knowledge and self-reliance.
- Modern educational reformers look to Tagore's model as a blueprint for creating inclusive and sustainable educational practices.

3. Aesthetic Theories
Tagore's Artistic Vision
- Tagore's artistic contributions, especially in the visual arts, reflect a blend of Eastern and Western influences. His paintings, characterised by their unique style and emotive power, challenge traditional art forms and invite contemporary analysis.
- Art historians and critics explore how Tagore's work prefigures modernist movements and contributes to a global understanding of aesthetics.

Music and Dance
- Tagore's compositions in Rabindrasangeet and his innovations in dance dramas like "Chitrangada" and "Shyama" continue to influence the Indian performing arts. His works integrate lyrical poetry, classical ragas, and traditional dance forms to create a distinctive artistic expression.
- Contemporary performers and choreographers draw from Tagore's repertoire to create new interpretations that resonate with today's audiences.

4. Social and Political Thought

Tagore on Nationalism and Internationalism
- Tagore's critique of narrow nationalism and his vision of a global human community are highly relevant in today's interconnected world. He advocated for a form of internationalism that respected cultural diversity while promoting universal values.
- Political theorists and global studies scholars examine Tagore's ideas to understand and address contemporary issues of nationalism, globalisation, and cultural diplomacy.

Environmental Thought
- Tagore's deep appreciation for nature and his advocacy for environmental conservation resonate with today's ecological concerns. His writings often reflect a symbiotic relationship between humans and the natural world.
- Environmentalists and sustainability advocates find in Tagore's works a philosophical foundation for promoting ecological balance and ethical environmental practices.

Key Essays and Discussions

Patrick Hogan's essay "Why Ratan Fell in Love Unnoticed and Why Ashu Was Ashamed: Tagore's Short Fiction and the Ethics of Feeling" explores the emotional and ethical dimensions of Tagore's short fiction, focusing on how his characters navigate personal and social dilemmas, delving into the psychological underpinnings of love, shame, and moral choices. Satadru Sen, in "Remembering Robi: Childhood, Freedom, and Rabindranath Tagore," reflects on Tagore's childhood experiences and their influence on his educational philosophies, highlighting how his early life shaped his ideas on freedom, creativity, and nurturing young minds. Monali Chatterjee's "The Delineation of the Female Subject in Rabindranath Tagore's Novel 'Farewell, My Friend'" provides insights into Tagore's portrayal of female autonomy and agency in "Shesher Kobita" (Farewell, My Friend), discussing how he navigates the tension between traditional gender roles and modern aspirations. Esha Niyogi De's essay "Gender, Nation, and the Vicissitudes of Kalpana: Choreographing Womanly Beauty in Tagore's Dance Dramas" examines the representation of women in Tagore's dance dramas, highlighting the complex interplay of gender, nationalism, and aesthetics, and discussing how his choreographic works challenge and redefine traditional notions of femininity and beauty.

Rabindranath Tagore's interdisciplinary legacy continues to inspire and challenge scholars, artists, educators, and social thinkers. His visionary ideas and creative expressions offer a rich tapestry for contemporary exploration and application. As we delve deeper into his works, we uncover layers of meaning and relevance that speak to the enduring quest for knowledge, beauty, and human connection in the 21st century.

Tagore's ability to transcend cultural, linguistic, and temporal boundaries makes him a timeless figure whose thoughts and works remain a beacon of intellectual and artistic inspiration. Whether through the lens of literary criticism, educational reform, aesthetic theory, or social and political thought, Tagore's contributions continue to resonate, offering profound insights and guiding principles for navigating the complexities of modern life.

8

Foundations of Tagore's Philosophy

Tagore's philosophical foundation is predominantly rooted in the Vedantic tradition, drawing significantly from the Upanishads and Buddhist teachings. He viewed these ancient texts not as relics of the past but as living spiritual forces that continue to grow and evolve. Tagore's reverence for the Upanishads and Buddha's teachings is evident in his writings, where he often infuses these philosophies with a personal and contemporary resonance.

We can see Tagore's philosophy as a restatement of ancient Indian wisdom, tailored to address the complexities of modern life. He believed that the spiritual insights of the Upanishads and Buddhism possess a boundless vitality, capable of providing guidance at any age. This belief reinforces his belief that spirituality and humanism are dynamic and evolving aspects of human existence, not limited to the past.

Tagore's Vision of Life and Humanity

Central to Tagore's philosophical vision is the concept of unity – the unity of the individual soul with the universal spirit, the unity of humanity, and the unity of man with nature. His idea of the "universal man," who transcends narrow identities and embraces a larger, spiritual identity, encapsulates this vision. From his poetry to his essays, Tagore's literary works mirror this vision, depicting a world where all forms of existence intertwine.

Tagore's idea of unity is not merely philosophical but also practical, influencing his educational and social initiatives. He founded Shantiniketan, an educational institution aimed at fostering holistic development, combining the best of Eastern and Western traditions. This institution was a microcosm of his vision for humanity – a place where individuals could grow in harmony with themselves, each other, and the natural world.

Poetry and Philosophy

For Tagore, poetry was not just an artistic pursuit but a profound expression of his philosophical thoughts. Deep philosophical insights imbue his poetic works like "Gitanjali" and "The Gardener," which explore themes of love, divinity, and the human condition. Through poetry, Tagore sought to bridge the gap between the finite and the infinite, capturing the sublime beauty of the spiritual experience.

Tagore believed that poetry had the power to touch the soul and communicate truths that transcended intellectual understanding. He viewed poetry as a means of expressing the ineffable, using its music and imagery to convey spiritual experiences. His poetry is a testament to his belief that beauty and truth are intertwined, and that the poetic imagination is a pathway to understanding deeper philosophical truths.

The Message to India

Tagore's writings and speeches often emphasised the need for inner freedom and spiritual awakening as prerequisites for true national freedom.

Tagore's vision for India was not just about political independence but also about cultural and spiritual rejuvenation. He believed that India had a unique spiritual heritage that could offer much to the world, and he worked tirelessly to promote this heritage through his writings and educational initiatives. His message to India was one of self-discovery and self-realisation, urging the nation to find its true identity by reconnecting with its spiritual roots.

The Message to the World

He was a vocal critic of nationalism and materialism, advocating instead for a global community bound by shared human values and mutual respect. His travels and interactions with the leading intellectuals of his time underscored his commitment to this ideal, promoting a vision of a world united by love and understanding.

Tagore's internationalism is evident in his numerous lectures and writings, where he often spoke about the need for a global consciousness that transcended national boundaries. He believed that humanity's true progress lay in its ability to recognise its shared destiny and work together for the common good. Tagore's vision of a world united by spiritual and cultural bonds remains a powerful counterpoint to the divisive forces of nationalism and materialism.

The Enduring Legacy

His emphasis on the spiritual dimension of life, the unity of all existence, and the transformative power of love and creativity offers a powerful antidote to the crises of modernity. As we navigate the complexities of the contemporary world, Tagore's wisdom serves as a guiding light, reminding us of the deeper truths that bind us together as human beings.

Tagore's legacy is not just in his writings but also in his educational and social initiatives, which continue to influence generations. Shantiniketan remains a living testament to his vision of holistic education, while his literary works continue to be read and appreciated worldwide. Tagore's philosophy, with its blend of ancient wisdom and modern insight, offers a timeless guide to living a meaningful and harmonious life.

9

Excerpts from Tagore's most famous creation, Gitanjali

Where the mind is without fear and the head is held high
Where knowledge is free
Where the world has not been broken up into fragments
By narrow domestic walls
Where words come out from the depth of truth
Where tireless striving stretches its arms towards perfection
Where the clear stream of reason has not lost its way
Into the dreary desert sand of dead habit
Where the mind is led forward by thee
Into ever-widening thought and action
Into that heaven of freedom, my Father, let my country awake.

Fun Fact:
Santiniketan's alumni, like Amartya Sen and Satyajit Ray, exemplify its legacy of excellence. The institution's open studios and artistic freedom continue nurturing creative minds, maintaining its influence and cultural significance.

This is my prayer to thee, my lord—strike, strike at the root of penury in my heart
Give me the strength lightly to bear my joys and sorrows.
Give me the strength to make my love fruitful in service.

Give me the strength never to disown the poor or bend my knees
before insolent might.
Give me the strength to raise my mind high above daily trifles.
And give me the strength to surrender my strength to thy will
with love.

I thought that my voyage had come to its end at the last limit of
my power,—that the path before me was closed, that provisions
were exhausted and the time come to take shelter in a silent
obscurity.
But I find that thy will knows no end in me. And when old words
die out on the tongue, new melodies break forth from the heart;
and where the old tracks are lost, new country is revealed with its
wonders.

Fun Fact:
Tagore integrated the Santhal tribal community into Santiniketan, fostering rural reconstruction. Today, Santiniketan is a major center for educated Santhals, many becoming teachers or social workers, reflecting Tagore's inclusive educational model.

That I want thee, only thee—let my heart repeat without end. All
desires that distract me, day and night, are false and empty to the
core.
As the night keeps hidden in its gloom the petition for light, even
thus in the depth of my unconsciousness rings the cry—I want
thee, only thee.
As the storm still seeks its end in peace when it strikes against
peace with all its might, even thus my rebellion strikes against thy
love and still its cry is—I want thee, only thee.

When the heart is hard and parched up, come upon me with a shower of mercy.
When grace is lost from life, come with a burst of song.
When tumultuous work raises its din on all sides shutting me out from beyond, come to me, my lord of silence, with thy peace and rest.
When my beggarly heart sits crouched, shut up in a corner, break open the door, my king, and come with the ceremony of a king.
When desire blinds the mind with delusion and dust, O thou holy one, thou wakeful, come with thy light and thy thunder.

The rain has held back for days and days, my God, in my arid heart. The horizon is fiercely naked—not the thinnest cover of a soft cloud, not the vaguest hint of a distant cool shower.
Send thy angry storm, dark with death, if it is thy wish, and with lashes of lightning startle the sky from end to end.
But call back, my lord, call back this pervading silent heat, still and keen and cruel, burning the heart with dire despair.
Let the cloud of grace bend low from above like the tearful look of the mother on the day of the father's wrath.

Where dost thou stand behind them all, my lover, hiding thyself in the shadows? They push thee and pass thee by on the dusty road, taking thee for naught. I wait here weary hours spreading my offerings for thee, while passers by come and take my flowers, one by one, and my basket is nearly empty.
The morning time is past, and the noon. In the shade of evening my eyes are drowsy with sleep. Men going home glance at me and smile and fill me with shame. I sit like a beggar maid, drawing my skirt over my face, and when they ask me, what it is I want, I drop my eyes and answer them not.
Oh, how, indeed, could I tell them that for thee I wait, and that thou hast promised to come. How could I utter for shame that I

keep for my dowry this poverty. Ah, I hug this pride in the secret of my heart.

I sit on the grass and gaze upon the sky and dream of the sudden splendour of thy coming—all the lights ablaze, golden pennons flying over thy car, and they at the roadside standing agape, when they see thee come down from thy seat to raise me from the dust, and set at thy side this ragged beggar girl a-tremble with shame and pride, like a creeper in a summer breeze.

But time glides on and still no sound of the wheels of thy chariot. Many a procession passes by with noise and shouts and glamour of glory. Is it only thou who wouldst stand in the shadow silent behind them all? And only I who would wait and weep and wear out my heart in vain longing?

Rabindranath Tagore Reading

> **Fun Fact:**
> In 1862, Maharishi Debendranath Tagore discovered Santiniketan, captivated by its serene landscape. He established a spiritual center for meditation across religions, naming it the 'abode of peace'. Rabindranath Tagore later founded an experimental school here in 1901.

Early in the day it was whispered that we should sail in a boat, only thou and I, and never a soul in the world would know of this our
pilgrimage to no country and to no end.
In that shoreless ocean,
at thy silently listening smile my songs would swell in melodies, free as waves, free from all bondage of words.
Is the time not come yet?
Are there works still to do?
Lo, the evening has come down upon the shore
and in the fading light the seabirds come flying to their nests.
Who knows when the chains will be off,
and the boat, like the last glimmer of sunset,
vanish into the night?

✺

The day was when I did not keep myself in readiness for thee; and entering my heart unbidden even as one of the common crowd, unknown to me, my king, thou didst press the signet of eternity upon many a fleeting moment of my life.
And to-day when by chance I light upon them and see thy signature, I find they have lain scattered in the dust mixed with the memory of joys and sorrows of my trivial days forgotten. Thou didst not turn in contempt from my childish play among dust, and the steps that I heard in my playroom are the same that are echoing from star to star.

✺

This is my delight, thus to wait and watch at the wayside where shadow chases light and the rain comes in the wake of the summer.
Messengers, with tidings from unknown skies, greet me and speed along the road. My heart is glad within, and the breath of the passing breeze is sweet.
From dawn till dusk I sit here before my door, and I know that of a sudden the happy moment will arrive when I shall see.
In the meanwhile I smile and I sing all alone. In the meanwhile the air is filling with the perfume of promise.

Have you not heard his silent steps?
He comes, comes, ever comes.
Every moment and every age,
every day and every night he comes, comes, ever comes.
Many a song have I sung in many a mood of mind,
but all their notes have always proclaimed,
'He comes, comes, ever comes.'
In the fragrant days of sunny April through the forest path he comes,
comes, ever comes.
In the rainy gloom of July nights on the thundering chariot of clouds
he comes, comes, ever comes.
In sorrow after sorrow it is his steps that press upon my heart, and it is the golden touch of his feet that makes my joy to shine.

> **Fun Fact:**
> Rabindranath Tagore envisioned education rooted in surroundings yet connected globally. He founded Brahmacharya Ashram in 1901, later Patha Bhavan. Classes held outdoors promoted harmony with nature, with students engaging in nature walks and studying life cycles.

I know not from what distant time thou art ever coming nearer to meet me. Thy sun and stars can never keep thee hidden from me for aye.
In many a morning and eve thy footsteps have been heard and thy messenger has come within my heart and called me in secret.
I know not why to-day my life is all astir, and a feeling of tremulous joy is passing through my heart.
It is as if the time were come to wind up my work and I feel in the air a faint smell of thy sweet presence.

The night is nearly spent waiting for him in vain. I fear lest in the morning he suddenly come to my door when I have fallen asleep wearied out. Oh friends, leave the way open to him—forbid him not.
If the sound of his steps does not wake me, do not try to rouse me, I pray. I wish not to be called from my sleep by the clamorous choir of birds, by the riot of wind at the festival of morning light. Let me sleep undisturbed even if my lord comes of a sudden to my door.

Fun Fact:
The ethos of Santiniketan, encapsulated in Tagore's vision of inclusive, holistic education, remains relevant today. The institution's commitment to traditional crafts, environmental sustainability, and cultural diversity preserves Tagore's visionary educational model.

Ah, my sleep, precious sleep, which only waits for his touch to vanish. Ah, my closed eyes that would open their lids to the light of his smile when he stands before me like a dream emerging from darkness of sleep. Let him appear before my sight as the first of all lights and all forms. The first thrill of joy to my awakened soul let it come from his glance. And let my return to myself be immediate return to him.

The morning sea of silence broke into ripples of bird songs; and the flowers were all merry by the roadside; and the wealth of gold was scattered through the rift of the clouds while we busily went on our way and paid no heed.

We sang no glad songs nor played; we went not to the village for barter; we spoke not a word nor smiled; we lingered not on the way. We quickened our pace more and more as the time sped by.

The sun rose to the mid sky and doves cooed in the shade. Withered leaves danced and whirled in the hot air of noon. The shepherd boy drowsed and dreamed in the shadow of the banyan tree, and I laid myself down by the water and stretched my tired limbs on the grass.

> **Fun Fact:**
> Tagore's legacy at Santiniketan is a testament to his belief in the transformative power of education. His vision of a place where the mind is free and knowledge unbounded continues to inspire and guide Santiniketan, making it a living embodiment of Tagore's ideals.

My companions laughed at me in scorn; they held their heads high and hurried on; they never looked back nor rested; they vanished in the distant blue haze. They crossed many meadows and hills, and passed through strange, far-away countries. All honour to you, heroic host of the interminable path! Mockery and reproach pricked me to rise, but found no response in me. I gave myself up for lost in the depth of a glad humiliation—in the shadow of a dim delight.

The repose of the sun-embroidered green gloom slowly spread over my heart. I forgot for what I had travelled, and I surrendered my mind without struggle to the maze of shadows and songs. At last, when I woke from my slumber and opened my eyes, I saw thee standing by me, flooding my sleep with thy smile. How I had feared that the path was long and wearisome, and the struggle to reach thee was hard!

> **Fun Fact:**
> Santiniketan, 158 km from Kolkata, embodies Tagore's vision of transcending barriers through education, evolving into Visva Bharati University in 1921. Established in 1863, it emphasizes humanism, internationalism, and sustainability, integrating nature, arts, and cultural exchange.

You came down from your throne and stood at my cottage door. I was singing all alone in a corner, and the melody caught your ear. you came down and stood at my cottage door.

Masters are many in your hall, and songs are sung there at all hours. But the simple carol of this novice struck at your love. One plaintive little strain mingled with the great music of the world, and with a flower for a prize you came down and stopped at my cottage door.

I had gone a-begging from door to door in the village path, when thy golden chariot appeared in the distance like a gorgeous dream and I wondered who was this King of all kings!

My hopes rose high and methought my evil days were at an end, and I stood waiting for alms to be given unasked and for wealth scattered on all sides in the dust.

> **Fun Fact:**
> Cricket Lover: Tagore was an avid cricket fan and even organized matches in Shantiniketan, encouraging students to play.

The chariot stopped where I stood. Thy glance fell on me and thou camest down with a smile. I felt that the luck of my life had come at last. Then of a sudden thou didst hold out thy right hand and say "What hast thou to give to me?"

Ah, what a kingly jest was it to open thy palm to a beggar to beg! I was confused and stood undecided, and then from my wallet I slowly took out the least grain of corn and gave it to thee. But how great my surprise when at the day's end I emptied my bag on the floor to find a least little grain of gold among the poor heap. I bitterly wept and wished that I had had the heart to give thee to my all.

Charulata, based on Rabindranath Tagore's novel Nastanirh
Credits: Satyajit Ray, CC BY-SA 4.0 <https://creativecommons.org/licenses/by-sa/4.0>, via Wikimedia Commons

The night darkened. Our day's works had been done. We thought that the last guest had arrived for the night and the doors in the village were all shut. Only some said, The king was to come. We laughed and said "No, it cannot be!"

It seemed there were knocks at the door and we said it was nothing but the wind. We put out the lamps and lay down to sleep. Only some said, "It is the messenger!" We laughed and said "No, it must be the wind!"

> **Fun Fact:**
> Japanese Inspiration: Tagore was profoundly influenced by Japanese aesthetics, which can be seen in his paintings and poetry.

There came a sound in the dead of the night. We sleepily thought it was the distant thunder. The earth shook, the walls rocked and it troubled us in our sleep. Only some said, it was the sound of wheels. We said in a drowsy murmur, "No, it must be the rumbling of clouds!"

The night was still dark when the drum sounded. The voice came "Wake up! delay not!" We pressed our hands on our hearts and shuddered with fear. Some said, "Lo, there is the king's flag!" We stood up on our feet and cried "There is no time for delay!"

The king has come—but where are lights, where are wreaths? Where is the throne to seat him? Oh, shame! Oh utter shame! Where is the hall, the decorations? Some one has said, "Vain is this cry! Greet him with empty hands, lead him into thy rooms all bare!"

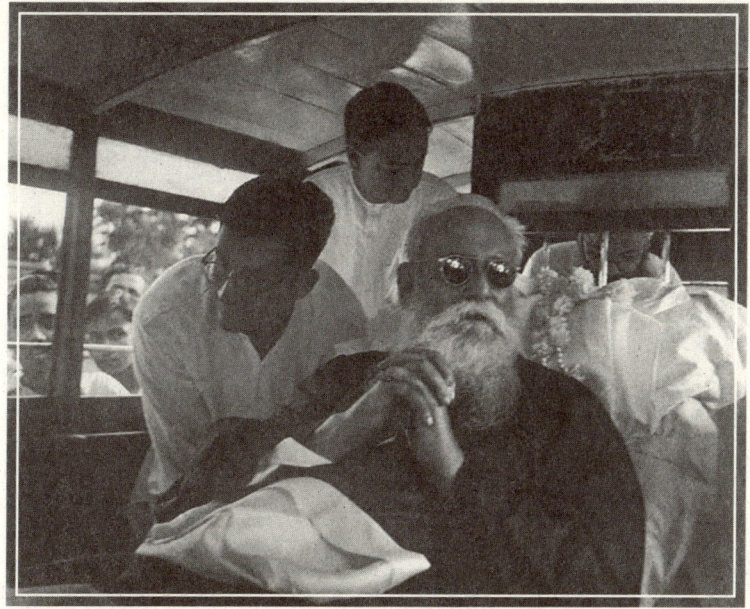

Tagore: His Last Journey

Open the doors, let the conch-shells be sounded! In the depth of the night has come the king of our dark, dreary house. The thunder roars in the sky. The darkness shudders with lightning. Bring out thy tattered piece of mat and spread it in the courtyard. With the storm has come of a sudden our king of the fearful night.

List of works

Poetry			
Bengali Title	Transliterated Title	Translated Title	Year
* ভানুসিংহ ঠাকুরের পদাবলী	Bhānusimha Thākurer Padāvalī	(Songs of Bhānusimha Thākur)	1884
* মানসী	Manasi	(The Ideal One)	1890
* সোনার তরী	Sonar Tari	(The Golden Boat)	1894
* গীতাঞ্জলি	Gitanjali	(Song Offerings)	1910
* গীতিমাল্য	Gitimalya	(Wreath of Songs)	1914
* বলাকা	Balaka	(The Flight of Cranes)	1916
Dramas			
* বাল্মিকী প্রতিভা	Valmiki-Pratibha	(The Genius of Valmiki)	1881
* কালমৃগয়া	Kal-Mrigaya	(The Fatal Hunt)	1882
* মায়ার খেলা	Mayar Khela	(The Play of Illusions)	1888
* বিসর্জন	Visarjan	(The Sacrifice)	1890
* চিত্রাঙ্গদা	Chitrangada	(Chitrangada)	1892
* রাজা	Raja	(The King of the Dark Chamber)	1910

* ডাকঘর	Dak Ghar	(The Post Office)	1912
* অচলায়তন	Achalayatan	(The Immovable)	1912
* মুক্তধারা	Muktadhara	(The Waterfall)	1922
* রক্তকরবী	Raktakarabi	(Red Oleanders)	1926
* চণ্ডালিকা	Chandalika	(The Untouchable Girl)	1933
Fiction			
* নষ্টনীড়	Nastanirh	(The Broken Nest)	1901
* গোরা	Gora	(Fair-Faced)	1910
* ঘরে বাইরে	Ghare Baire	(The Home and the World)	1916
* যোগাযোগ	Yogayog	(Crosscurrents)	1929
Memoirs			
* জীবনস্মৃতি	Jivansmriti	(My Reminiscences)	1912
* ছেলেবেলা	Chhelebela	(My Boyhood Days)	1940

Adaptations of novels and short stories in cinema and TV		
Bengali		
Natir Puja	1932	The only film directed by Rabindranath Tagore
Naukadubi	1947	Nitin Bose
Bou Thakuranir Haat	1953	Naresh Mitra
Kabuliwala	1957	Tapan Sinha
Kshudhita Pashaan	1960	Tapan Sinha
Teen Kanya	1961	Satyajit Ray
Charulata	1964	Satyajit Ray
Ghare Baire	1985	Satyajit Ray
Chokher Bali	2003	Rituparno Ghosh
Shasti	2004	Chashi Nazrul Islam
Shuva	2006	Chashi Nazrul Islam
Chaturanga	2008	Suman Mukhopadhyay
Noukadubi	2011	Rituparno Ghosh
Elar Char Adhyay	2012	Bappaditya Bandyopadhyay
Hindi		
Sacrifice	1927	Nanand Bhojai and Naval Gandhi
Milan	1946	Nitin Bose
Dak Ghar	1965	Zul Vellani
Kabuliwala	1961	Bimal Roy
Uphaar	1971	Sudhendu Roy
Lekin...	1991	Gulzar
Char Adhyay	1997	Kumar Shahani
Kashmakash	2011	Rituparno Ghosh
Stories by Rabindranath Tagore (Netflix)	2015	Anurag Basu